THE LITTLE GUIDE TO DOLLY PARTON

UNOFFICIAL AND UNAUTHORISED

MIX
Paper | Supporting
responsible forestry
FSC® C020056

FSC
www.fsc.org

Published in 2022 by OH!
An Imprint of Welbeck Non-Fiction Limited,
part of Welbeck Publishing Group.
Based in London and Sydney.
www.welbeckpublishing.com

ISBN 978-1-91161-038-0

Compiled by: Malcolm Croft
Editorial: Victoria Godden
Project manager: Russell Porter
Design: James Pople
Production: Freencky Portas

A CIP catalogue record for this book is available from the British Library

Printed in China

10 9 8

Jacket cover photograph: Everett Collection Inc/Alamy Stock Photo

THE LITTLE GUIDE TO DOLLY PARTON

IT'S HARD TO BE A DIAMOND IN A RHINESTONE WORLD

CONTENTS

INTRODUCTION

In March 2020, Dolly Parton, at the grand ol' age of 74, told the world she wanted to pose on the cover of *Playboy* magazine (again). This request, in many ways, perfectly sums up the Dolly Parton we all know and love – the big boobin', bleach-blonde wig-wearin', Southern hillbilly-in', rhinestone-rubbin' rube. And yet, paradoxically, it's nowhere close to defining the *real* Dolly.

Since her arrival to Nashville, in 1964, with her uncle Bill Owens and big dreams of country music superstardom, Dolly's rags-to-riches yarn made her instantly relatable to her all-American fans, even when her "cheap whore" appearance told a different story. But, even then, aged just 18, Dolly was double-daring her audience to not judge books by their covers, even if those covers are 48DDs in size.

While the pens of writers, journalists and critics have run dry of adjectives, hyperbole and crass comments to describe this near-dollar billionaire country bumpkin, Dolly herself has thankfully yet to run out of wise, witty words and countless quips and quotes to describe herself and her awesome life in music, hence the necessity for this tiny tome in your home. Her famous Dollyisms – bitesize positive life affirmations and thigh-slappin' wisecrackin' one-liners – are as adored and as well-travelled as her heartbreakin' and love-makin' lyrics.

So, we're all in agreement, then: A life without Dolly Parton is no life at all. Dolly, we will *always* love you.

CHAPTER

ONE

HELLO, DOLLY!

In the 1960s US music industry,
Dolly was as rare as the
rhinestones she often ridiculously
revered. Her emergence onto
the country (and then pop)
scene started a revolution and
gave Dolly (and all the females
who followed her) a voice for
the first time.
When Dolly sang, doors opened.
Say hello to Dolly…

"

I've just been dragged screaming
and kicking into the 21st century.
But I try to surround myself
with folks that keep up with it.
It's completely different now. It's
wonderful that I'm still here.

"

**Reflecting on her long career during
an interview with Matt Lauer on the
Today Show, 13 May 2014**

> **"** When I talk to a man, I can always tell what he's thinkin' by where he's lookin'. See, if he's lookin' at my eyes, he's lookin' for intelligence. If he's lookin' at my mouth, well, he's lookin' for wit and wisdom. If he's lookin' anywhere else except my chest... he's lookin' for another man. **"**

**Reflecting on her ability to read men
in a TV interview with Michael Parkinson,
17 September 2007**

“

I'm sure there's lots of people out there who'd like to smack my head off, but we won't talk about them. I've lived a lot and I've done a lot. People relate to me because I grew up poor and in a big family. They know I understand all the hardships.

”

Reflecting on her relatability in an interview with *Billboard*

" Some people didn't think I was a class act because of my looks. But it didn't take them long to find out they were wrong. **"**

Reflecting on her signature style in an interview with the *Daily Mail*

" Our house had running water, if you were willing to run and get it. **"**

Reflecting on her "dirt poor" upbringing in an interview with *Stylist* magazine

66

I've got too much to lose – like my hair! Lord knows what else could fall out of me.

99

Discussing having never ridden any of Dollywood's rollercoasters in an article with *USA Today*

66

I'd be disappointed if I went somewhere and nobody noticed me.

99

Reflecting on her fame in an interview with _Hot Press_

> **"**
> I don't know what 'Goin'
> Hollywood' means; if it means goin'
> to shit, no.
> **"**

**Discussing her move away from
country music in an interview
with *Rolling Stone***

"

I often say I don't lose my temper, but sometimes I have to *use* my temper.

"

Reflecting on her early career performance in an interview with *NME*

"

I landed my first gig, in Knoxville, at the Cas Walker live music radio show. Cas said hello and stared down at me like he expected me to say something back. I said, 'Mr Walker, I want to work for you.' He shook my hand and said, 'You're hired. A lot of people come to me and say, "Mr Walker, I want a job," but you're the first one that ever said, "I want to work." '

"

Discussing her first gig in an article with *Guideposts*

"

Am I livin'? Am I a legend? You never know how people are going to look at you till you're older and you look back at your life. So far I've been very pleased that, you know, my life has turned out the way it has, and I don't take it for granted. I owe a lot of credit to God and folks for helping me along the way, so I didn't do this all by myself.

"

**Reflecting on her status as a "living legend"
in an interview with *Mashable***

" I'm a vanilla sinner – too bad to be good and too good to be bad. **"**

Discussing sins in a 1977 interview with *Rolling Stone*

" People hopefully now at least know there is a heart beneath the boobs and that's one of the reasons my boobs are so big, it's just all heart pushin' out my chest. **"**

Discussing her 48DD breasts in an interview with *Bust* magazine

"

The only way I'd be caught without make-up is if my radio fell in the bathtub while I was taking a bath and electrocuted me and I was in between make-up at home. I hope my husband would slap a little lipstick on me before he took me to the morgue.

"

Discussing her make-up requirements in an interview with Oprah Winfrey

---

"

When it's more than I can stand,
I just get my pencil and guitar out
and I start writin'.

"

**Discussing songwriting in a 1977
interview with *Rolling Stone***

"

To me, when I talk about not being a natural beauty – I'm not. Trust me when I say: In the mornings, I gotta get up and paint on stuff. Those people who wake up and they're just beautiful, they're just born that way. Well that ain't me. I gotta work for everything I've got.

"

Discussing her looks in an interview with
Southern Living

" I would have been a great mother. I would probably have given up everything else. I probably wouldn't have been a star. **"**

On never having children, in an interview with *The Guardian*

"

My lawyers and my accountants and a lot of people that I was working with at the time said I was making a big mistake. But I just knew it was right and… I got rid of all those people, started over with new people that did believe in my dreams.

"

On never giving up her Dollywood dreams, in an interview with ABC News video, conducted by Robin Roberts, for the ABC News special "Dolly Parton: Here She Comes Again!"

"

I say that I'm as old as yesterday, but hopefully as new as tomorrow.

"

Reflecting on her long career during an interview with Matt Lauer on the *Today Show*

" We all need to have hope that there's something bigger than we are. Even if I knew for a fact that there was no God, I'd still believe. **"**

Reflecting on her life philosophy during an interview for the *Oprah Magazine*

"

Wigs are just so handy. I never have a bad hair day, and that's a good thing.

"

Reflecting on her hair pieces in an interview with *Elle* magazine

66

I do the best I can every day, and I'm going to enjoy my life. Some people work at being miserable. I work at being happy.

99

Reflecting on her life philosophy during an interview for the *Oprah Magazine*

"

I always wore tight clothes.
When I walked down the hall,
everybody was a-lookin' to see
how tight my skirt was that day or
how tight my sweater was. I never
did like to go around half-naked
but a lotta people said I might
as well be naked, as tight as my
clothes were.

"

**Reflecting on her distinctive look in a
1977 interview with *Rolling Stone***

" I've lived a lot in my time. I said I was married, I didn't say that I was dead. **"**

Reflecting on her personal life in an interview with _Hot Press_

"

I love the tabloids; I believe everything in them about everybody but me.

"

Reflecting on her tabloid perception in an interview with *The Times*

" It takes all of this to be me; this is how I think I look my best. **"**

Reflecting on her distinctive look in an interview with the BBC

"

You think boobs, you think
Dolly Parton.

"

**Discussing her breasts in an interview
with *Chicago Tribune*, 1 April 1992**

"

If I had it to do all over, I'd do it all over again. I'm dragging him kicking and screaming into the next 50 years. Wish us luck.

"

**Discussing celebrating her
50th wedding anniversary in
an interview with *E Online***

"

My first thought was 'I'm gonna marry that girl.' My second thought was, 'Lord she's good lookin.' And that was the day my life began. I wouldn't trade the last 50 years for nothing on this earth.

"

Carl Dean Thomas, discussing celebrating their 50th wedding anniversary in an interview with *E Online*

" I graduated from high school on a Friday night in 1964. On Saturday morning I left for Nashville, never to come back. **"**

Reflecting on her move to Nashville in an interview with the *New York Times*

"

I'm not going to limit myself just because people won't accept the fact that I can do something else.

"

A famous Dollyism, posted by Dolly to her Twitter page, 3 November 2010

> **"** I've been around a long time. Long enough for people to realise that there's more to me than the big hair and the phoney stuff. **"**

On her reputation, in an interview with *The Guardian*

"

I don't think people can live in this world without going through times. People always look at me, [and] they always say, 'Oh, you just always seem to be so happy.' I said, 'That's the Botox.'

"

On her positivity, in an interview with ABC News video, conducted by Robin Roberts, for the ABC News special "Dolly Parton: Here She Comes Again!"

" If I'm not a good example of a woman in power, I don't know who is. I don't have to preach. I write it. I sing it. I live it. I'm out there just promoting mankind, but I am most definitely going to get behind those gals. **"**

Discussing gender equality in an interview with *Elle* magazine

"

If you don't like the road
you're walking, start paving
another one.

"

**A famous Dollyism, posted by Dolly to
her Twitter page, 20 June 2014**

"

I'll be this way when I'm 80, like Mae West. I may be on crutches, in a wheelchair or propped up on some old slantboard, but I'll have my high heels, my nails and make-up on, my hair'll be all poufed up and my boob'll still be hangin' out. It's not a big job being Dolly. It's just my life.

"

Discussing her plans not to retire in an interview with *Ladies Home Journal*

CHAPTER

TWO

JOLLY DOLLYISMS

Throughout Dolly's long and winding career, she has become as famous for her quick wit and wisecrackin' humour – adored as 'Dollyisms' – as much as her record-breakin', heartachin' music. If you're lookin' for a slice of country wisdom, salvation lies within…

"

I know every line in his face and he knows every hair in my wig.

"

Discussing her husband Carl Thomas Dean during an interview with Matt Lauer on the *Today Show*, 13 May 2014

> **"** If I had chosen the name Dolly Dean… I'd have been Double D. Again! **"**

On why she didn't take her husband's name, in an interview with *The Guardian*

"

I'm a songwriter, so I have to live with my feelings on my sleeve. I have to not harden my heart, because I want to stay open to feel things. So when I hurt, I hurt all over. And when I cry, I cry real hard. And when I'm mad, I'm mad all over. But I was born with a happy heart. I'm always looking for things to be better.

"

Reflecting on her positive outlook in an interview with *Southern Living*

"

I'm more successful now than I was then, but I still feel like the same girl. I'm just a working girl. I never think of myself as a star because, as somebody once said, 'A star is nothing but a big ball of gas' – and I don't want to be that.

"

Reflecting on her fame in an interview with *Billboard*

"

I believe that without God I am
nobody, but that with God,
I can do anything.

"

**Reflecting on her faith in an interview
with Roger Ebert**

"

I am sure of myself as a person. I am sure of my talent. I'm sure of my love for life. I am very content. I like the kind of person that I am. So, I can afford to piddle around and do-diddle around with make-up and clothes and stuff because I am secure with myself.

"

Discussing her confidence with her appearance in a 1977 interview with Barbara Walters

" You have to be really strong to avoid temptation in this business and even if you don't avoid it you have to be smart enough to know how much of it you can take. **"**

Discussing the music industry in a 1977 interview with *Rolling Stone*

"

What I lack in talent I make
up for in ambition and faith and
determination and positive
thinking.

"

**Discussing the power of positive thinking
in a 1977 interview with *Rolling Stone***

> **"**
> I never let a rhinestone go
> unturned!
> **"**

A famous Dollyism posted by Dolly to her Twitter page, 11 March 2015

"

I wake up with new dreams
every day.

"

**Discussing the power of dreams in an
interview with *Mashable***

"

I can just see two big mountains growing up out of my grave, and people going around on mule rides to look at them.

"

Discussing her legacies in an interview with Reuters

"

I grew up poor, so poor my daddy paid the doctor who delivered me with a sack of cornmeal.

"

Discussing her "dirt poor" upbringing in an article with *Guideposts*

"

My weaknesses have always been food and men – in that order.

"

A famous Dollyism, posted by Dolly to her Twitter page, 18 February 2013

"

I may be a pioneer, but I'm blazing new trails all the time, so don't give up on me.

Discussing her long career in an interview with *The Tennessean*

"

If you've been fortunate enough to see dreams come true, in my case I have, but I paid my dues. I always say I'm going to give God the credit but I definitely want the cash.

"

Reflecting on her dream career in an interview with *Digital Journal*

66

I was looking up at the big sign that says Hollywood, and I thought, 'Wouldn't it be great if someday I could jerk that big ol' H down and put a D there to make it Dollywood?' Eleven years ago I got to see that dream come true in the mountains.

99

Discussing the genesis of Dollywood in an interview with *Country Weekly*

"

I've never thought of myself as a
feminist. I've used my femininity and
my sexuality as a weapon and a
tool … but that's just natural.

"

**Reflecting on her sexuality in an
interview with *The Times***

> When I'm inspired, I get excited because I can't wait to see what I'll come up with next.

A famous Dollyism, posted by Dolly to her Twitter page, 6 April 2015

" I don't know if I'm supporting them or they're supporting me. "

Reflecting on her breast size in an interview with *The Star*

66

There's only one sort of exercise I like and it ain't jogging. If I jogged I'd end up with two black eyes.

99

Reflecting on her fitness regime in an interview with *The Times*

"

It's been such a thrill for me tonight to see all these great artists singing songs I've written or been a part of. Watching them is sort of like watching porn. You're not personally involved but you still get off on it.

"

Discussing live cover performances of versions of her own songs when accepting MusiCares Person of the Year award

DOLLY PARTON

"
There are going to be those who will say, 'I know that they're false; I knew her when…' and there will be some who say, 'I know they're real.' I say: 'Let 'em guess.'

Reflecting on rumours of breast implants in a 1977 interview with *Rolling Stone*

66

Now people are always asking me,
'What do you want people to say
about you 100 years from now?'
I always say I want them to say,
'Dang, don't she still look good for
her age.'

99

**Discussing her legacy in her 2009
University of Knoxville commencement
speech**

DOLLY PARTON

" I want people to know it's me when they see me coming and when they see me leavin', so I figured I might as well look even more extreme. **"**

Discussing her distinctive look in *Dolly on Dolly: Interviews and Encounters with Dolly Parton*, edited by Randy L. Schmidt, Chicago Review Press

"

I've said that I had to get rich in order to sing like I was poor again. But I count my blessings more than I count my money.

"

Reflecting on her wealth in an interview with *Hot Press*

"

I've got to do so many things: movies, records, write songs for movies, do some business things, Dollywood, but still, music is right in the heart of it.

"

Reflecting on her long career in an interview with *Rookie* magazine

THREE

RAGS TO RICHES

Dolly Parton was born on
19 January 1946 in a one-room
cabin on the banks of the
Little Pigeon River in Pittman
Center, Tennessee. From these
humble beginnings, Dolly learnt
the true meaning of life – and
she's been teaching it to all of
us, through her songs and her
wisecracking wit, every
day since.

"

In the winter time, we just had a pan of water and we'd wash down as far as possible, and we'd wash up as far as possible. Then, when somebody cleared the room, we'd wash 'possible'.

"

Discussing her "dirt poor" upbringing with journalist Lawrence Grobel for *Playboy*'s March 1978 issue

> **"** Ever since I was little, I've been like a horse with blinders. I didn't hear a voice, but it was a knowing that came to me, and it said, 'Run. Run until I tell you to stop.' And that's what it's been, I've kept on keeping on. And I never let a person, nor a thing, nor a sickness, nor a heartache, nor anything keep me from keeping on. **"**

Reflecting on her ambition in an interview with *The Guardian*

"

Don't get so busy making a living that you forget to make a life.

"

One of Dolly's famous Dollyisms, posted by Dolly to her Twitter page, 9 August 2010

"

I met him the day I got to Nashville back in 1964. I wasn't a star then, so I've never had to worry that he loves me because I'm a star and I've got money or make money or whatever. I know he loves me for me, and that means a lot to me.

"

Discussing her successful marriage in an interview with Oprah Winfrey

"

My songs are like my children and I expect them to support me when I'm old.

"

Discussing her songs in an interview with *Bust* magazine

"

I ain't near where I'm goin'. My dreams are far too big to stop now 'cause I ain't the greatest at what I do, but I become greater because I believe.

"

Discussing the power of dreams in a 1977 interview with *Rolling Stone*

"

I've got better things to do than count them. But I wear one every day of the week, so probably 365.

"

Discussing how many wigs she owns in a July 1984 interview with *Interview* magazine conducted by Andy Warhol and Maura Moynihan

" God tells us not to judge one another, no matter what anyone's sexual preferences are or if they're black, brown or purple. And if someone doesn't believe what I believe, tough shit. **"**

Reflecting on her tolerance in an interview with *The Guardian*

"

The way I look was really a country girl's idea of what glamour was. I patterned my look after the town tramp. I thought she was the prettiest thing in the world, with all that bleached hair and bright-red lipstick. People would say, 'Oh, she's just trash,' and I'd think, 'That's what I want to be when I grow up.'

"

Discussing her signature look in an interview with *Rolling Stone*

> "I wrote 'I Will Always Love You' straight from the bottom of my heart. You hope that songs are hits. You have no way of knowing."

Reflecting on hit songs in an interview with *Larry King Live*

> **"** I was the first woman to burn my bra, it took the fire department four days to put it out. **"**

A famous Dollyism, posted by Dolly to her Twitter page, 30 April 2010

66

I have no taste. But I know good taste when I see it. I appreciate it and respect it. I just don't know how to do it.

99

Discussing her distinctive look in an interview with *USA Today*

"

I've dreamt myself into a corner.
People say, 'Oh, you could quit
work.' I say, 'No, I couldn't. I've got a
family to feed. I've got dreams
to dream.'

**Reflecting on retirement in an interview
with *The Times***

> **"**
>
> Some people are just born cussers.
> I don't even realise I'm doing it.
> If I have offended anybody …
> tough titty.
>
> **"**

Reflecting on her love of swearing in an interview with _The Times_

" People always ask me how long it takes to do my hair. I don't know, I'm never there. **"**

Reflecting on her distinctive appearance in an interview with *Harper's Bazaar*

" I never met a man whose rear I couldn't kick if he didn't treat me with the right respect. **"**

Discussing her career when accepting the MusiCares Person of the Year award

"

You think she's here – but she ain't!

"

Reflecting on what she'd like written on her tombstone in an interview with *Hot Press*

"

I got songs stuck everywhere. I pull out a drawer to get some panties. I'll find a song in there.

"

Reflecting on her prolific approach to songwriting in an interview with Dan Rather

"

Being a star just means that you just find your own special place and that you shine where you are.

"

Reflecting on fame in an interview with *Interview* magazine conducted by Andy Warhol and Maura Moynihan

"

When I was a teenager I
wrote a lot of real hot and heavy
love stories, I was just so
horny myself.

"

**Discussing her teenage desires in a
1977 interview with *Rolling Stone***

"

If I have one more facelift, I'll have a beard.

"

Discussing plastic surgery in an interview with *Bust* magazine

> **"**
> I know some of the best
> Dolly Parton jokes. I made 'em up
> myself.
> **"**

**Discussing her perception in the press in
an interview with Roger Ebert**

"

I've been fortunate in my life that my being a girl kind of helped me along the way, and being from a strong family of men, and women, I'd never be afraid to stand on my own or to say, 'Go to hell', if that's where you needed to go.

"

Reflecting on her femininity in an interview with *Elle* magazine

> **"** The magic with me is that I look completely false when I'm completely real. **"**

Reflecting on her looks and personality in an interview with *The Guardian*

"

I try to encourage women
to be all that they can be and
I try to encourage men to let
us be that.

"

Discussing feminism in an interview with
***Bust* magazine**

" I make a better whore than a secretary. **"**

Discussing her role in *Nine to Five* in an interview with *Interview* magazine conducted by Andy Warhol and Maura Moynihan

"

I don't know one thing or another about fashion, but people know I'm gonna dress the way I dress.

"

Reflecting on her fashion sense in an interview with *The Guardian*

"

In the early days, there was no technology. I started writing songs because we didn't have a chance to go to movies and we didn't have TV, so I would write songs, just make up stories that were really kind of like movies, and I would sing them. It was entertainment to us.

"

Reflecting on her early songwriting days in an interview with *Cosmopolitan*

"

If something sounds familiar, I think, 'Oh my goodness, what is that?' Then I'll track it down and, in my case, it's usually just one of my own songs!

"

Discussing plagiarism in an interview with the BBC

"

I wake up every day expecting things to be good and if they're not, I set about trying to make them as good as I can. By the end of the day, I like to feel like I've tried to do my best and make that day as good a day as I can make it.

"

Reflecting on her life philosophy in an interview with *Digital Journal*

"

There are 24 hours in a day, 365 days a year. You should be able to get everything done and just be smart about it.

Reflecting on her desire to work in an interview with *Metro Sunday*

"

If it hadn't been for music, I'd have been
a beautician… Even if I wasn't in show
business, I would have wanted all the
glamour – and that's about the only
way a girl in a small Southern town
is going to get it, being a beautician.
Or maybe I'd have been a missionary;
I thought about that too, but where
would I get my hair done?

"

**Reflecting on an alternative career in an
interview with the *Saturday Evening Post*, 1989**

"

You think you'd run out of stuff to write about, the same melodies, the same storylines, but there's always a little twist in everything.

"

Reflecting on having written more than 5,000 songs in an interview with *Rookie* magazine

" I've been in business for 40 years. I've won everything you can win, I've had hit records, I've got to travel, I've made good money. But I still don't feel like I'm done though. **"**

Reflecting on her longevity in an interview with _Hot Press_

FOUR

HILLBILLY HEARTBREAKER

Dolly may not allow the roots
on her wigs to show, but when it
comes to the roots of where she
came from – the Great Smoky
Mountains – Dolly could not be
prouder of her provenance.
And it taught her a thing or
two about how to live, love and
laugh. Truths she now passes
on to you…

"

I'm not admitting nothin'. Maybe I did. Maybe I didn't. Maybe I will. Maybe I won't. And it's none of your damn business!

"

On tabloid rumours, in an interview with
The Guardian

"

I've always believed in my talent. And I've always had more guts than talent.

"

On her determination, in an interview with *Southern Living*

"

I don't care how ugly I get as long as I'm healthy. I figure my best years are goin' to be between 50 and 100.

"

Discussing the longevity of her looks in a 1982 interview with *People* magazine

> **"**
>
> I always felt like I was somebody special, maybe it's because I needed to be somebody special. I just always knew I was going to be a star. **"**

Discussing her fame in an interview with *Interview* magazine conducted by Andy Warhol and Maura Moynihan

❝

I'm outgoing on the inside, so I felt I needed to be as flamboyant on the outside.

❞

Reflecting on why she feels compelled to look the way she does in an interview with *The Times*

> The way I see it, if you want the rainbow, you got to put up with the rain.

A famous Dollyism, posted by Dolly to her Twitter page, 17 February 2015

"

Carl says he'd think less of any man who didn't fall in love with me.

"

Discussing her marriage in an interview with the *Daily Mail*

"

After you reach a certain age, they think you're over. Well, I will never be over. I'll be making records if I have to sell them out of the trunk of my car. I've done that in my past, and I'd do it again.

"

Reflecting on her age in an article by *Harper's Bazaar*

"

I surround myself with great people, because I know what I know, and I know what I don't know.

"

Discussing "Team Dolly" in an interview with *InStyle*

66

If something is bagging, sagging
or dragging, I'll tuck it, suck it or
pluck it.

99

**Reflecting on her plastic surgery
in an interview with *The Guardian***

" I think the way I have conducted my life and my business and myself speaks for itself. I don't think of it as being feminist. It's not a label I have to put on myself. **"**

**Reflecting on feminism in
an interview with *The Guardian***

> **"**
> When I went to Nashville they liked my personality, and I never sold myself out. I never went to bed with anybody unless I wanted to, never for business reasons. **"**

Reflecting on her early career in an interview with *Interview* magazine conducted by Andy Warhol and Maura Moynihan

"

Every now and then when I'm with my husband I'll think, 'Yeah, I'll make love with Burt Reynolds tonight' – as long as it ain't Burt. My old man don't know about it, but I'm sure he wouldn't mind. I'm sure he makes love to many people while I'm the one doin' all the work.

"

Discussing fantasises in a 1982 interview with *People* magazine

"

I do just as I please, I always have and always will. I try to live my own life; I don't try to live somebody else's life, and I don't like people tryin' to live my life.

"

Detailing her life philosophy in a 1977 interview with *Rolling Stone*

"

It's a very simple melody, really easy to sing, like holding the notes. Even if you can't sing, you can sing, 'Iiiiiiiiii-Iiiiii will alwaaaaays love yooou'. Plus there's a message. I think everybody can connect with it, whether it's their lost love affair, or a partnership, or when children go off to college, or when people die.

"

Reflecting on the success of "I Will Always Love You" in an interview with *Bust* magazine

"

My nails are my rhythm section,
when I'm writing a song all alone.
Someday, I may cut an album, just
me and my nails.

"

**Discussing her songwriting in an
interview with Roger Ebert**

"

I've always been misunderstood because of how I look. Don't judge me by the cover 'cause I'm a real good book!

"

On people's first impressions, as posted by Dolly on her Twitter page, 25 November 2014

66

I hope to fall dead on stage right in the middle of a song – and hopefully one I wrote.

99

On her last moments, in an interview with CMT

66

In the South, we're very famous for porches. You get outside and sit on your porch – that's where you do your biggest dreaming.

99

On daydreaming, in an interview with *Southern Living*

" I'm not leaving the country, I'm just taking it with me. **"**

Discussing her move away from country music in a July 1984 interview with *Interview* magazine conducted by Andy Warhol and Maura Moynihan

---

"

I love getting on a big writing binge and staying up a couple days working on a song and knowing at the end of those two or three days that I've created something that was never in the world before.

"

Reflecting on her songwriting process in an interview with *American Songwriter*

"

I have a good sense of humor,
and I'm pretty witty myself.
Like, 'It costs a lot of money to
look this cheap!' I say that over and
over, year after year, and people
laugh. Oh, heavens, I've been using
that line over 25 years!

"

**Discussing her sense of humour
in an interview with *Vogue***

"

When I was 35, it was a pinnacle, a great time in my life – success and happiness and all that. And so I just decided, 'I'm gonna claim that number and always be that in my state of mind.'

"

Reflecting on her career in an interview with the BBC

"

I was surprised and delighted that while he talked to me, he looked at my face – a rare thing for me. He seemed to be genuinely interested in finding out who I was and what I was about.

"

Reflecting on meeting her husband in a press release for Dolly and Carl's 50th wedding anniversary

" People know I have no taste. No style. No class. If I have any class, it's all low. No matter how I dress, I'm still going to look cheap. **"**

Discussing her distinctive look in an interview with *The Times*

"

If it hadn't been for my Backwoods Barbie syndrome, I would probably have had no one paying that much attention to me as a songwriter. I would never have even got the chance to get my foot in the door if I hadn't been a freak to start with.

"

Reflecting on her distinctive look in an interview with *The Sun*

"

We hillbillies may not have sex,
drugs and rock 'n' roll, but two out
of three ain't bad.

"

**Discussing her career when accepting
MusiCares Person of the Year award**

"

I think of myself as somebody who's just as smart as any man I know. I don't think anybody should ever be judged by whether they're male or female, black, white, blue, or green. I think people should be allowed to be themselves and to show the gifts they have and be able to be acknowledged for that and to be paid accordingly.

"

Discussing her affection for the LGBTQ+ in an interview with *Bust* magazine

> **"**
>
> I was walking down the street to the laundromat, and he stopped me. He said, 'Hey, you're going to get sunburned out here!' Well, he had to say something.
>
> **"**

On how she met her husband, in an interview with *The Guardian*

"

God's like a farmer. He gets up
and throws out all of these ideas
like corn, and I want to be the
early bird.

"

**On songwriting, during an interview for
the *Oprah Magazine***

FIVE

QUEEN
OF COUNTRY

Dolly's songs are the soundtrack to
several generations of souls who have
loved her music and lyrics ever since
her first single 'Puppy Love' back in
1959, released when she was just 13.
Skip forward a few years, and
Dolly is now the queen of country,
the grandmother of gospel and the
world's longest reigning ruler of
rock-a-billy-roll, selling more than
160 million albums. In that time, she's
learnt all the tricks and secrets of
the trade…

"

I don't care what people say about me, good or bad. I mean, you'd like them to say everything good, but I wouldn't want to be that vanilla. Through the years, people must think I've really got around. I guess I have, to some degree.

"

**On criticism, in an interview with
*The Guardian***

66

I mean we were really Hill. Billies. To me that's not an insult. We were just mountain people. We were really redneck, roughneck, hillbilly people. I'm proud of my hillbilly, white trash background. To me that keeps you humble; that keeps you good. And it doesn't matter how hard you try to outrun it – if that's who you are, that's who you are.

99

Reflecting on her "hillbilliness" in an interview with *Southern Living*

"

I really wish that y'all could have seen the look on my lawyer's face 24 years ago when I told him I wanted to start a theme park and call it Dollywood. He thought I'd already taken the train to Crazywood.

"

Discussing the creation of Dollywood in her 2009 University of Tennessee commencement speech

"

I would never stoop so low to be fashionable, that's the easiest thing in the world to do. I don't like to be like everybody else.

Discussing her distinctive look in a 1977 interview with Barbara Walters

"

I feel that sin and evil are the negative part of you, and I think life is like a battery: you've got to have the negative and the positive in order to be a complete person.

"

Discussing sin in an interview with *Interview* magazine conducted by Andy Warhol and Maura Moynihan

"

If my attitude needs more adjusting, I visualize God holding me upside down and shaking all the negative stuff – fears, doubts, insecurities – right out of me. Try it. Ask God to turn you upside down! It's a sure-fire pick-me-up.

"

Discussing her relationship with God in an article by *Guideposts*

"

Don't want to see, don't want
to know.

"

**Reflecting on the current colour of her
hair in an interview with *The Times***

"

When I'm a little bit bad, I have a
chat with God, ask his forgiveness
and then go straight back out there
and party again.

"

**Reflecting on her relationship with
God in an interview with *The Times***

"

I hope people see the brain underneath the wig and the heart beneath the boobs.

"

Discussing her distinctive look in an interview with George Stroumboulopoulos for CBS News

"

I'd collect my brothers and sisters who were too young to run away, sit them down in the dirt, then get up on the porch and belt out songs into a tin can on a stick like I was at the Grand Ole Opry. If I couldn't round up any of my brothers and sisters, there were always the pigs and chickens to serenade.

"

Discussing her first audience in an article by _Guideposts_

"

I look just like the girl next door…
if you happen to live next door to
an amusement park.

"

**Reflecting on her distinctive appearance
in an article by *Harper's Bazaar***

"

People take me as seriously as I want them to. They take me as seriously as I take myself — let's put it that way. I think I'm fun for other people, and an unusual kind of package. That I can look totally artificial and be totally real is perfectly fine with me.

"

Reflecting on her signature look in an interview with the *Chicago Tribune*, 1992

"

I'm comfortable in my own skin, no matter how far it's stretched.

"

Reflecting on her distinctive look in an interview with *The Times*

"

Find out who you are and do it
on purpose.

"

**A famous Dollyism, posted by Dolly
to her Twitter page, 8 April 2015**

"

When you do something that great, it's really hard to try to go back and top it. And I've kind of always had a philosophy that I don't chew my tobacco more than once.

"

Reflecting on her career longevity in an interview with *Larry King Live*

" Through the years, I've always used my femininity to my benefit. I've never slept with anybody to get to the top, though. If I slept with somebody, it's 'cause I wanted to, not to get from point A to point B. **"**

Discussing men in an interview with *Bust* magazine

"

I just kind of over-exaggerated everything I am – bigger hair, bigger beauty mark, bigger boobs, if you can imagine.

"

Discussing the time she came second in a Dolly lookalike contest in an interview with Oprah Winfrey

> **"** You can wish your life away. But if you're going to dream, you're going to have to get out and put some wings on them dreams, and some feet and fingers and some hands. You can't just sit around and think of all the things you want to do. You've got to think of what you want to do, and then you've got to get out and make that happen. **"**

Reflecting on her determination to become a star in an interview with _Southern Living_

"

I usually try not to give advice.
Information, yes; advice, no. But
what has worked for me may
not work for you. Well, take for
instance what has worked for me.
Wigs. Tight clothes, push-up bras,
and high-heel shoes.

"

**Discussing her signature look in her 2009
University of Tennessee commencement
speech**

"

I'm flashy, and I'm flamboyant. To me, that's still one of the funniest things, when people say that I am a fashion icon.

"

Discussing her status as a fashion icon in an interview with *Elle* magazine

66

Lord, I've been around for so long that people looked at me like a legend. But when I turned 35 I wasn't near done. I felt like I was better than I ever was. And I thought, 'Well, hell, I'm not going down with the rest of them old farts. I'm gonna find some new ways of doing it.' And that's exactly what I did.

99

Discussing her career longevity in an interview with *Rolling Stone*

DOLLY PARTON

> **"** One of my first hit records was called 'Dumb Blonde' and that's kind of followed me around over the years. But the song says just because I'm blonde, don't think I'm dumb, because this dumb blonde ain't nobody's fool. I'm a fool sometimes but I'm not fool enough to talk politics, so what else you got? **"**

Reflecting on her desire to not express her political opinions in an interview with *Hot Press*

"

I guess you could say I created this person, this character. And I like her. I mean, the image is something I made up, but it's not like the image is separate from me. I still know who the little girl from Sevier is. I never lose sight of her.

"

**Discussing her "Dolly Parton"
persona in an interview with *McCalls***

"

Everything's a song to me. Anything that happens, any conversation I have, somebody'll say somethin', I think, 'Oooh, that's a good idea for a song.'

Reflecting on her prolific approach to songwriting in an interview with Dan Rather

SIX

LIVIN' DOLL

"I really don't think about my age. If my health holds up I'll still be doing this at 95, if I live that long."

So said Dolly, regarding her age in an interview with *Glamour* magazine. Today, Dolly is an icon of music and culture, a global superstar who will always be loved as a livin' legend. And you don't become a legend without learning a thing or two…

"

I am totally real, as a writer, as a professional, as a human being. A rhinestone shines just as good as a diamond.

"

On her realness, in an interview with *Elle* magazine

"

If they ask me, I just say,
'Yeah, whatever. And I ain't
done yet!'

"

**On plastic surgery, in an interview
with *Southern Living***

"
Are they real? They're real
expensive. They're real big.
"

**Reflecting on the size of her 48DD
breasts in an interview with *USA Today***

"

I just wanted to be pretty. I wanted to be striking. I wanted to be colourful. I wanted to be seen. When I went to Nashville, I always overdid it. When they say, 'Less is more,' I say, 'That's BS. More is more.'

"

On her distinctive look, in an interview with *Elle* magazine

> "
>
> I had grown up in a family of men, with six brothers, my dad, my uncle, and my grandpa, who I loved dearly. I understood and knew the nature of men, so I had no fear of working in that world, because I understood it.
>
> "

Reflecting on the male-dominated music industry of the 1960s and 1970s in an interview with *Elle* magazine

"

I never felt I belonged. Never belonged in my whole life, even as a little kid. I was just different and so I never really found my place till I moved to Nashville and got in the music business. That was my real place, so I fit in.

"

Discussing her early career in a 1977 interview with *Rolling Stone*

66

I thought about bein' a stripper.
But I had my songs to sing, I had an
ambition and it burned inside me.
It was something I knew would
take me out of the mountains. I
knew I could see worlds beyond
the Smoky Mountains.

99

**Reflecting on her career choices in
a 1977 interview with *Rolling Stone***

> "
>
> I took up guitar at age seven, making my first instrument out of an old mandolin and two bass strings. I put on concerts right on our porch. To look the part of a glamorous singer, I used Mercurochrome for lipstick, crushed pokeberries for rouge and a burnt match for mascara.
>
> "

Discussing her discovery of musical instrumentation in an article by *Guideposts*

" It could be worse. They could tell the truth about me. **"**

Discussing her relationship with the tabloid press in an interview with *McCalls*

"

It's very hard for me to love a little, have sex a little, to eat a little. I like to do everything, and I like to do it all the way that I want to do it.

"

Discussing her passion for life in an interview with *Interview* magazine conducted by Andy Warhol and Maura Moynihan

"

I don't want someone to see
me and be disappointed. What
they're seeing reflects the phony
that I am.

"

**Discussing her distinctive look
in an interview with George
Stroumboulopoulos for CBS News**

"

When people started changin' their hair styles, I wasn't ready to quit – I just kept makin' it bigger and bigger. I just thought, well, somebody is noticin' it and I'm enjoyin' it. But people come to expect that of me and I come to expect it of myself, the flashy clothes and jewellery and all the gaudy appearance. I guess I did invent that part of me.

"

Reflecting on fashion choices in a 1977 interview with *Rolling Stone*

66

You're only going to know as much as I'm going to tell you.

99

Reflecting on privacy in an interview with *The Guardian*

"

A lot of people say to me, 'There are so few worthwhile people in the world,' and I say, 'That's the biggest crock of shit I ever heard.' I don't ever meet a freak. The biggest freaks in the world for me are my favourite people, like you, like me.

"

Reflecting on her tolerance in an interview with *Interview* magazine conducted by Andy Warhol and Maura Moynihan

"

I always just thought if you see somebody without a smile, give 'em yours!

"

On positivity, posted by Dolly to her Twitter page, 29 May 2014

"

I like to give it all away so that I have reason to work.

"

Discussing her wealth in an interview with *Interview* magazine conducted by Andy Warhol and Maura Moynihan

"

Take it from me, though, the fancy make-up is just highlighting what's for real. And that's true happiness, the kind that comes from the inside.

"

Discussing happiness in an article by *Guideposts*

"

The only advice I'd give would be
the advice I follow myself: To thine
own self be true.

"

**Reflecting on her life philosophy during
an interview for the *Oprah Magazine***

> **"**
>
> I don't need a therapist, 'cos I write it out. If I've got something bothering me, I just get it out. If I'm mad, I write that. If I'm hurt, I write that. If I'm happy, I write that. I write what I feel. That's my doctor. **"**

Reflecting on her songwriting as therapy in an interview with _The Times_

I've always been proud that I was born a woman, and I've joked that if I wasn't, I would have been a drag queen. That's my favourite line, but it's probably true.

Reflecting on being a woman in an interview with *Glamour* magazine

"

I was fourth down, with a sister and two brothers older than me and eight kids younger. Mamma and Daddy loved us all the same, but you know they didn't have time to do whatever. You had to work to get attention. So I started writing and singing.

"

Reflecting on her early singing career in an interview with *The Times*

" I'm my own boss, so I'm the only one I tell to kiss my ass. **"**

Reflecting on being in charge of many businesses in an interview with *Metro Sunday*

"

I'll always be too much for some people. But I'll never be enough for me.

"

Discussing her personality in an interview with *TV Guide*

Amy Loves the Rain

by Julia Hoban

pictures by Lillian Hoban

Harper & Row, Publishers

For Elizabeth

Library of Congress Cataloging-in-Publication Data
Hoban, Julia.
   Amy loves the rain.

   Summary: Amy and her mother drive through the rain to
pick up Daddy.
   [1. Rain and rainfall—Fiction.   2. Parent and
child—Fiction]   I. Hoban, Lillian, ill.   II. Title
PZ7.H63487Af 1989   [E]   87-45851
ISBN 0-06-022357-X
ISBN 0-06-022358-8 (lib. bdg.)

1 2 3 4 5 6 7 8 9 10
First Edition

118239

Amy Loves the Rain

It is a rainy day.
Amy sits in her car seat.

Let's pick up Daddy, Amy,
so he doesn't have to walk in the rain.

It is warm in the car on a rainy day.

The windshield wipers go *swish swak*.

The raindrops patter *pit pat*.

The car goes through a puddle—*splash plash*.

The sky is gray.

The streets are black and shiny.

The traffic light shines in the puddles.
Bright red, bright green.

Look, there is a man with a big umbrella.

Amy has an umbrella too.

Does Daddy have an umbrella?

No, he forgot his.

Daddy holds a newspaper over his head.

Amy, give Daddy your umbrella,

and he will give you a hug.